All the Queen's Horses

ALL THE QUEEN'S HORSES

A Celebration of
Her Majesty's Love of the Horse

David Elliott

AQS PUBLISHING
LONDON

Contents

Introduction

All The Queen's horses may not have been able to help Humpty-Dumpty be put back together, but their presence in an immortal nursery rhyme does, at least, suggest their magnificence. We are more fortunate in this Golden Jubilee Year, for during the 16th and 18th of May, 2002, a splendid entertainment will take place each evening in the Home Park of Windsor Castle, hosted by the Royal Windsor Horse Show.

Against the magnificent backdrop of a floodlit Windsor Castle, a fifty-foot high Lion and Unicorn, from the Royal Coat of Arms, will frame a stage with one of the largest outdoor lighting and sound rigs ever constructed. Over 100 musicians, a choir of 200 and multi-screen archived film presentations will compliment the greatest live equestrian stage show ever mounted, featuring 1,000 horses and 2,000 men, women and children. This spectacular celebration of The Queen's Golden Jubilee will culminate in a breathtaking recreation of the Coronation procession, using the Gold State Coach pulled by eight grey horses - a sight not seen since the 1977 Silver Jubilee.

This book is a modest contribution to that celebration.

It has been said that the Royal Windsor Horse Show is unique because of its setting and the close involvement of the Royal Family ever since the Show's modest beginnings. This book has greatly benefited from the access given its publishers to the extensive pictorial archives of the Show, kept in its offices in a quiet close, next to the Royal Mews at Windsor Castle. Many of the more personal and charming photographs which run as a *leitmotif* throughout the book's text come from there.

Sadly, we learned of the death of Princess Margaret as the collation of the photographs was beginning and it was during the very final stages of the book's production that the unhappy news of the death of the Queen Mother was announced. Although a few changes have been made to the text, it was felt that its spirit of celebration should not be altered.

·CHAPTER ONE·

BEGINNINGS

*King George VI at the
Royal Windsor Horse Show in 1945*

It was her grandfather, George V, who gave The Queen her very first 'horse', a Shetland pony called Peggy. The Queen was just four years old. King George V was extraordinarily fond of his grand-daughter. The Countess of Airlie, Lady-in-Waiting to Queen Mary, remembered that 'Lilibet always came first in his affections. He used to play with her - a thing I never saw him do with his own children – and loved to have her with him'. (King George V called the Duchess of York 'Lilibet', after she had become his daughter-in-law. By all accounts, the King was enchanted by his son's new bride, even allowing her to be late for a meal and meeting her apology with: 'We must have sat down a little early today'. Some biographers tell that Princess Elizabeth called herself 'Lilibet' when she first started to talk. Whatever the reason, 'Lilibet' would become Princess Elizabeth's affectionate nickname within the Royal Family and for those around them.)

It was reported that every morning, whilst the King was in residence at Buckingham Palace, and after he had lit his first cigarette of the day, he would look from his window to check the weather, then take a pair of binoculars and focus them at a top story window, across Green Park, where his grand-daughter would wave back at him. The Duke and Duchess of York and their two daughters lived at 145, Piccadilly.

The young Princess even stayed with the King whilst he convalesced in Bognor from a severe operation on his lungs. Her presence, everyone felt, had a remarkable affect on his recovery. King George V would also take the young Princess for walks on Sunday

*Queen Elizabeth awards a winner at the
Royal Windsor Horse Show in 1946*

afternoons to the Royal Stud at Sandringham, the King's favourite residence. Though her grandfather seemed more fascinated by the Navy or his stamp collection, rather than with the Turf (unlike his own father, Edward VII) there can be little doubt that The Queen's clear and certain love for all things equestrian started at a very, very early age, and her grandfather's influence would seem to have been rather important.

Her first proper riding lessons were with Horace Smith, whose riding school was near to the Royal Lodge in Windsor Great Park. Mr Smith would recall The Queen telling him, aged only thirteen, what she would have liked to have been, had not circumstance, tradition and duty carved another, more onerous, route out for her:

The Princess Elizabeth with her pony, photographed on her 13th birthday at Windsor, April 21st 1939

Princess Elizabeth would have liked 'to be a lady living in the country, with lots of dogs and horses'. (The Queen's first corgi was given to her when she was seven, three year's *after* the pony!)

Marion Crawford ('Crawfie'), who was governess to the two princesses and an intimate of the Royal Household for nearly twenty years (until she wrote about it) claimed that Princess Elizabeth's 'first love of all was undoubtedly Owen, the [Buckingham Palace] groom, who taught her to ride'. If the royal governess is to be believed, the young princesses would climb upon her back, place a pretend bit in her mouth and ride her round the nursery. 'Crawfie' also described a game Princess Elizabeth would play before bedtime: 'She used to tie the cord of her dressing-gown to a knot on her bed and drive an imaginary horse twice round an imaginary park, before going to sleep'.

Another nightly ritual would be the unsaddling and grooming of the many toy horses which the Princess had been given, as gifts over the years of her childhood and early adolescence. Indeed, it seems that a long line of toy horses, possibly, if some sources are correct, as many as thirty, remained in a row, complete with removable saddles and blankets, outside her bedroom at Buckingham Palace, until she left it to be married.

One of The Queen's biographers, Roland Flanini, claimed 'in later life, she would say that all the happiest memories of her childhood were associated with Windsor Castle and the Great Park, where she had the greatest pleasure horse riding'.

King George VI with Princess Elizabeth and Princess Margaret riding in Windsor Great Park, April 1938.

Certainly her mother, when Duchess of York, told Lady Cynthia Asquith that the young Princess would read and re-read 'anything we can find about horses and dogs'. The main attraction at Madame Tussaud's during the mid 1930s was an accurately crafted wax statue of the Princess Elizabeth sitting on her favourite pony.

By her early teens, Princess Elizabeth was a much accomplished rider, already taking an interest in her father's racehorses and seemed happiest when out riding or helping in the stables, working with and talking to the horses. At the very first Royal Windsor Horse Show in 1944, the Princesses Elizabeth and Margaret took part in the Single Private Driving Class competition. Princess Elizabeth took the reins, with her sister as passenger, in a pony phaeton which had been specially built for Queen Victoria's personal use, riding around the grounds in Windsor (and would eventually end up at Balmoral). The Princess drove a Norwegian pony, called Hans, and they won First Prize.

George VI's horse trainer, Fred Darling, reported that Princess Elizabeth had 'a natural eye for a horse'. And her obsession would last. In 1984, whilst on holiday in Wyoming, The Queen wrote a letter to the then American President, Ronald Reagan. She was, The Queen wrote, 'doing things I like best – looking at beautiful thoroughbreds...'.

The Monarchy and the horse have enjoyed a close and often much entwined relationship for many centuries. William Rufus was killed out hunting; when Henry VIII met his French counterpart near Calais on 'The Field of Gold', both monarch's horses were draped from ears to tail in a specially constructed blend of gold fabric and armour so heavy it took many men to get both Kings simply mounted, let alone met; Wat Tyler *knelt* as his young king rode out to meet him and his peasant army at Blackheath; Elizabeth I addressed her troops at Tilbury, sitting, we are told, side-saddle as she enthused them for the coming battle against the Spanish.

Queen Elizabeth awards a prize while The King and the two Princesses watch events in the ring at Windsor, 1946

Princess Elizabeth at the Windsor Show, 1945

The two Princesses walk out in the sunshine at the Windsor Horse Show, 1947

Indeed, the idea of monarch and animal has even reached a mythic dimension. The large man-made grass mound named Silbury Hill in Wiltshire is older even than the Great Pyramid. It's the largest paleontological structure in all of Europe and was constructed, so many believe, as a tomb built around the heroic body of a great dead king, sitting upon his favourite horse, with his sword held up above his head, ready to spring into action once more when the time was right. And it is, perhaps, appropriate, that we begin this celebration of all The Queen's horses with those the monarch uses for the great ceremonial functions of the Royal year. The horses and carriages which are kept in the Royal Mews at Buckingham Palace.

Pictured, left to right: Geoffrey Cross, Princess Margaret, Princess Marina, The King, The Queen, Duke of Beaufort and Princess Elizabeth at Windsor, 1946

The Royal Windsor Horse Show Scrapbook 1944-1946

The Royal Windsor Horse Show Scrapbook 1947-1949

·CHAPTER TWO·

THE ROYAL MEWS

*The Queen at the Royal Windsor
Horse Show, May 2000*

When George IV ascended the throne in 1820 he sought the services of John Nash and commissioned the aging architect to alter what was then called Buckingham House into a far grander and larger royal residence, fit to be called a palace. Part of the tired old man's brief was to alter the existing stables and after a three-year wait, the Royal Mews as we can still see it today with its two great Doric matching arches, was completed.

The first Royal Mews was built by Edward I during the 13th century, just up from the River Thames, near to Westminster at Charing Cross, on a site which is now part of the National Gallery. The buildings housed the King's collection of hunting falcons, and it is from the expression to keep a bird 'mewed up' that the collective noun for a place where horses, stables, carriages and often living accommodation are housed together, came into common usage. 'Mewing' is the name given to a natural process by which a falcon changes its plumage and the birds would be kept 'mewed-up' in their cages until their *mue* (an Old French word based on the Latin verb, *mutare* – to change) had been completed.

During the Middle Ages both king and nobility were fanatical falconers and the sport persisted for many centuries as a royal past-time. Three centuries later, Henry VIII would still 'mew' at Charing Cross, but when a fire in 1537 destroyed his stables in Bloomsbury (then called Lomesbury), he moved out his falcons, moved in his horses and the name stuck as the horse increasingly took over from the bird in social, and sporting, importance.

The Royal Mews was built during the reigns of Edward VI and Queen Mary but, as other monarchs altered or built other royal properties – we shall read later on, for example, of the magnificence of James I's palace at Newmarket – the Charing Cross buildings fell into disrepair. In 1732 , George II would develop the site once more to

*Finishing
Touches*

house his growing collection of horses. In 1760, his son, George III, bought some land from the Duke of Buckingham and moved his carriages – he liked collecting them – and attendant animals and humans to buildings at the back of Buckingham House. He built an indoor riding school in 1764 and renamed the new complex the Royal Mews, Pimlico. It was a busy place, by the sound of things. In 1785, the porter was instructed 'to suffer no loose, idle or suspicious persons, or women of the town to lurk or harbour near the Mews and to shut the gate at ten at night'.

And though the weathercock above the entrance porch still proudly displays the date, 1825, for the completion of Nash's conversion, work continued under other monarchs. William IV introduced gas lighting and flag-stoned the stable floors. Queen Victoria – the first monarch to make Buckingham Palace an official residence *and* a home – required the staff of the Royal Mews to take an even greater responsibility for maintaining the sovereign's livery and equestrian transportation. And with Prince Albert ever seeking to improve things, a new forge was built (the Prince kept his own horses stabled here) and even a cow took up occupation in a shed at the back, resulting in that part of the Royal Mews still being known as 'The Farm'. By 1859 the staff, and their families, had grown to nearly two hundred persons and new rooms were built above the stables and the coach-houses to accommodate them

Nowadays forty people, many with long-standing family connections with the Royal Mews, maintain a rigorous daily schedule to keep the horses, tackle and carriages all in tip-top condition. Traditions still remain, despite the five Rolls Royces and three Daimlers which, also under the auspices of the Royal Mews department, now convey The Queen and other members of the Royal Family to most of their official engagements. Since 1843, a Brougham has tripped lightly each day into the increasingly fraught London traffic, to collect and deliver the mail between the various royal households. And even though e-mail encroaches, the tradition remains. As does collecting and delivering back again the many foreign ambassadors from their various official residences to attend their audiences with The Queen at Buckingham Palace. The two state landaus, with attendant coachmen and footmen dressed in appropriate livery, first pick up the Marshal of the Diplomatic Corps, from St James's Palace, and then progress to the embassy to collect the ambassador. 'The aim,' maintains Paul Almond, who assists the Crown Equerry by managing the Royal Mews day by day, 'is to ensure that the ambassador arrives at Buckingham Palace at 11.57a.m. precisely – whatever the traffic is like outside'. It is an operation conducted with military precision.

A 'very superb' Gold State Coach was commanded to be made in 1762, for George III. It has been used in every coronation since George IV and was re-gilded to celebrate The Queen's Silver Jubilee, although special tests had to be carried out to ensure that the Coach could travel as far as St. Paul's Cathedral without mishap.

The Gold Coach passes by Buckingham Palace during the Silver Jubilee celebrations, 1977

It originally was driven by six horses with a coachman from the box, and the two leading horses postilion-ridden. King Edward VII considered this arrangement hindered the public's view and ordered the hammercloth and box removed. Ever since then the magnificent coach is drawn by eight postilion horses, whose red and gilt harness is as wonderful as their postilion's red and gold livery. The Irish State Coach was rebuilt after fire damage in 1911, and this is the coach which The Queen uses for the State Opening of Parliament. Queen Alexandra's State Coach always goes ahead, however, carrying the Imperial State Crown to the Palace of Westminster, which The Queen wears during that historic ceremony.

The elegant Scottish State Coach has been fitted with a glass roof which allows people watching above street level to see inside this lightest of all The Queen's

coaches. It was chosen to convey The Queen on her 60th Birthday to St George's Chapel, Windsor, and the Queen Mother journeyed in it to The Queen's Silver Jubilee Service. Road tests were not necessary. The 1902 State Landau was built for Edward VII and is painted in a lighter maroon than the other coaches. The coach, nearly always ridden open, drawn by six postilion horses, is normally used when The Queen must meet a foreign head of state, though both the Prince of Wales and Prince Andrew returned to Buckingham Palace, with their respective brides by their side, in it.

The Australian State Coach was presented to The Queen in Canberra on May 8th, 1988, to celebrate Australia's Bi-centennial year. The cost was met from public subscription and it was built, apart from the blue upholstery, supplied from the

The Irish State Coach enters the ring at Windsor

*Princess Elizabeth returns to Buckingham Palace
after attending the Trooping of the Colour ceremony, June 1947*

Royal Household and the exterior lamps from Ireland, with components construct-ed from materials entirely Australian. It was first used in October that year, when The Queen travelled in it to open Parliament. Perhaps the Glass Coach is the very daintiest of them all, bought for George V's coronation in 1911. It can be driven by as few as two horses, and has the largest glass windows of all the State coaches. The Queen returned from her wedding in it, as did Princess Anne. The Town Coach was restored in 1964, when what had been known as King Edward VII's Town Coach was fitted with larger windows. It is not as pretty as the Glass Coach, and like all the other State Coaches, can only proceed at a walking-pace.

The Queen rides down the Derby race-course

There are eight State Landaus still in use, the oldest one being built in 1838, the year of Queen Victoria's coronation. Five Semi-State Landaus, which were Queen Victoria's favourite choice of carriage, are also maintained in good working order, as are the five Ascot Landaus, kept at Windsor. These are the lightest and smallest of all the royal Landaus and are sometimes referred to as Pony Landaus. They are always used to convey The Queen and other members of the Royal Family up the course at the Royal Ascot race meeting. Smaller carriages – Barouches, Broughams, Clarences, Sociables, Phaetons, Victorias, Chaises, and more – are all maintained in first rate condition. Many of the carriages in the Royal Mews are rare and beautiful examples of the finest craftsmanship, and some have very special connections with The Queen's forefathers (and foremothers). A Pony Phaeton, for example, was espe-cially built to convey the very lame and obese King George IV, as he could, in his old age, no longer mount the steps of taller royal carriages.

The oldest Sociable kept in the Royal Mews bears this inscription: 'Lucerne St. Gothard Pass Furca Rhone Glacier Engelberg Augt. & Septr. 1868'. 'My own dear Scotch sociable was at the station', wrote Queen Victoria in her journal after arriving at Lucerne, 'driven from the box with four horses by a local coachman'. The Queen travelled 'straight up into the splendid mountains' and though it was sometimes 'miserably cold and cheerless', the royal party carried on. At Engleberg the going got rough. 'It is an unpleasant, tedious, nervous road, so rough and narrow. Brown, who is always so attentive and watchful, got out and walked near the carriage whenever we came to particularly steep and precipitous parts.'

The harnesses used at the Royal Mews, and the collection is almost certainly one of the finest in the world, date back in many instances, to the time when the coaches were built. There are eight sets of State harness, each one used for individual coaches, with the Number One State Harness only ever used for the Gold State Coach. There are also different liveries for the Royal coachmen and postilions. Ascot Livery is scarlet, purple and gold – The Queen's racing colours. State Livery is scarlet and gold with white silk stockings and ostrich feathered tricorne hats worn over white wigs. Semi-State Livery boasts a scarlet frock-coat, blue knee-breeches and a gold-laced top-hat. The horses are not forgotten either. The eight-piece red morocco State Harness was made in 1834; each piece weighs 110 lbs (242 kilos) and the rich ornamentation is of gilt ormolu.

According to the Royal Website, thirty-five horses live at the Royal Mews. 'Each horse is treated very much as an individual,' says Paul Almond. 'The Queen has a keen interest in horses and the work of the mews and names all her carriage horses herself.' The set of eight grey horses which draw The Queen's carriage are named Auckland, Iceland, Dresden, Alderney, St Patrick, King's Troop, Jubilee and Britannia. Every horse is carefully attended to. Barbados, a Cleveland Bay, has an aversion to blankets and so installed in his stall are special heat lights to ensure he does not catch cold. Their training is intense, for not only must the horses deal with traffic and often tight negotiations in transit, they also must deal with noise, brass bands, very bright ceremonial colours and crowds of people. It is a lengthy and precise process.

Horses are chosen when they are around three years old. Tapes of military music and pieces of coloured material are gradually brought to bear in the horse's training routine, as are difficult manoeuvres, though the horse does not progress to a carriage for at least six months, being led from the rein till then. Acquainting the horse to working in traffic is experimented with, to begin with, cautiously. It is only when everyone is sure that the horse can cope with the pressure of it all that the animal will be introduced to its new role in carrying out official duties. It is a process which takes around four years. And the upkeep must also be as painstaking. Horses have to be re-shoed every four weeks; London's roads are hard and wearing. All saddlery is hand-stitched and all the carriages must be maintained in full working order. Even, the web-site tells us, the leather tops of the coachmen's boots are maintained within the confines of the Royal Mews. Much progress has certainly been made since the bleak and rationed days of The Queen's coronation. Then some horses had to be rented back from the film producer Alexander Korda, who had bought them from the Royal Mews, in the much darker times of the Second World War, as so many men in the Royal Household had to take on the more pressing burden of defending

The Queen and Prince Phillip leave Buckingham Palace in the Irish State Coach to perform the first State Opening of Parliament of her reign, November 1952. This photograph was chosen as the image for the first stamps to be issued in The Queen's reign.

these shores. (And this, despite the gift of horses from Queen Wilhelmina of the Netherlands, given as a token of gratitude for the Royal Family's wartime help to her and the Dutch royal family.)

There are Royal Mews at Windsor Castle, and the buildings which house the Royal Mews at the Palace of Holyrood in Edinburgh, are amongst the oldest parts of the Palace. Both are still very much working environments, even when The Queen is not in residence. The office of Master of the Horse in the Royal Household is an ancient and important one. The first, John Russell, was created by Richard II in 1391 and a record of this high-ranking appointment (it ranks next to the Lord Chamberlain and the Lord Steward) has existed ever since then. The first Crown Equerry, Major John Richard Groves appointed in 1854, was also Secretary to the Master of the Horse, as well as Superintendent of the Royal Mews.

Although the Master of the Horse would stop having any direct administrative role in the managing of the Royal Mews, he still attends The Queen as her senior personal attendant when horses are used for any state occasion. The current Master of the Horse, Lord Vestey, took up the post in 1999. His predecessor, Lord Somerleyton, an officer in the Coldstream Guards, was also an accomplished point-to-point rider and was Master of the Waveney Hunt for sixteen years. It may be pertinent to note that Lord Somerleyton's grandfather was a Lord-in-Waiting to King

The Queen rides in Windsor Great Park with Prince Charles and Princess Anne, 1956

On the way to the Palace

George V, reflecting, perhaps, the tradition of maintaining connections between generations of monarchs and royal servants. This touching tradition has borne considerable achievements in Estate management, landscape gardening and many other aspects of the Royal environment, but perhaps the greatest achievements have been seen in the traditions and relationships which created, and still maintain today, the remarkable legacy of the Royal Studs.

The Royal Windsor Horse Show Scrapbook The 1950s

The Royal Windsor Horse Show Scrapbook 1960-79

·Chapter Three·

'The Glorious Uncertainty of the Turf'

The Queen at Windsor, 1995

On the day of her coronation, and probably to lighten what must have been a somewhat tense time, one of The Queen's Ladies-in-Waiting asked her if everything was going smoothly. Her Majesty reportedly replied that everything was indeed in good order. Her horse trainer, Cecil Boyd-Rochfort, had telephoned her that morning from Sandringham and told her that Aureole, a horse for whom there was great expectations, perhaps even winning the Derby, had performed very well in his last work-out.

The role of the English monarch in the development of the Thoroughbred horse is a long and fascinating one. King Athelstan, the grandson of Alfred the Great, was the first English sovereign to own racehorses, and horseraces were held usually at the festivals of Easter and Pentecost. There were annual races at Chester and it is well recorded that just a few months before coming to the throne in 1377, Richard II rode there against the Earl of Arundel. He won. In King John's Register of Royal Expenditure, clear expenses are shown incurred by the running of horses and both Edward II and III actually bred horses. It was Henry VIII, however, who started the first Royal Stud in much the same way as he started quite a few other things. The increasing wealth which came from commerce and expanding European trade provided the monarch with both the power and, more importantly perhaps, the need to be seen to have the best of everything there was.

The horse was essential both as a symbol of power, but also as a vital component within the manipulation of that power. The acts of ceremony, battle, communication, movement and even leisure were unthinkable without the equestrian relationship of man, some women, and the horse. It was vital that the English monarch

*Medieval
knight in
armour at the
Windsor Horse
Show*

sought to own the finest horses and so inevitable that amongst all the other requirements of the royal household, there would be the creation of a stud. Henry's first one was at Eltham, were a royal palace had stood for many years. In 1514 and 1515 Barb horses were imported from the Duke of Mantua. And even when Henry was in pursuit of new wives, his equestrian ambitions were not forgotten. Though he did not get his bride this time, Charles V of Spain gave him twenty-five Spanish horses, instead of his daughter, the Infanta. By 1531 there were studs at Tutbury, in Staffordshire and at Cole Park, Malmesbury – one of the richest and most important monasteries soon to be acquired during the dissolution of the monasteries between 1533 and 1536. In a royal inventory of the same date, the King owned eighty-five horses spread between the two royal establishments.

Under Queen Elizabeth I, and at her specific request, Robert Dudley, Earl of Leicester instigated a report on stud management from one of the greatest exponents in breeding studs and horses at that time, Prospero d'Osma. He was from Naples, then one of the great equestrian centres of Europe. Prospero sailed over to England in 1576 to discover that whilst there were over sixty mares at Malmesbury and twenty mares at Tutbury, the Queen owned no stallion. Prospero reported to Earl Dudley that 'if a stallion is given proper care, he can cover twelve mares (much to his pleasure) without suffering any damage. Calculating twelve mares to each stallion, I reckon six stallions will be enough for Her Majesty's entire stud'.

By the time Elizabeth died, race-meetings had become frequent events at Chester, Doncaster, York, Croydon, Richmond (in Yorkshire), Lincoln, Carlisle and

Salisbury. There were even races held in St. James's Park in London. The Queen, herself, attended races at Croydon in May 1574, 1585, 1587 and 1588, but it was her successor, James I, who first showed that epic adoration of the Turf that earned the act of horse-racing its eternal *homage* as 'the sport of kings'. James had already written of his obsession. In his defence of his own Divine Right, a book called 'Religio Regis or the Faith and Duty of a prince,' the King wrote: 'The honourablest and most commendable Games that a King can use are on Horseback, for it becomes a Prince above all men to be a Good Horseman'. He built a palace at Newmarket, to be near to the race-course and when twelve members of Parliament went there to petition the King to turn 'against too much sport and too little business of state', he threw them out. He did not even allow his Queen's death on March 1st 1619 to stop him attending the Spring race-meeting at Newmarket on the 19th.

James appointed George Villiers, Duke of Buckingham to be his Master of the Horse and the Duke did well. 'God thanke,' wrote King James, 'the maister of the horse for provyding me such a number of faire usefull horses'. Not that George Villiers did not miss any opportunity to strengthen his own stud which he established at Helmsley in Yorkshire, especially when generous monarchs gave gifts. In 1623 the King of Spain gave twenty-four horses, several mares and some foals from his stud at Cordova and Villiers ensured he took his 'commission'.

The Queen, watched by her mother and sister, greet Aureole after it won at Royal Ascot in June, 1954

James's son, Charles I, inherited his father's passion. A foreign diplomat was to write of the new King's hospitality at Newmarket that in the palace 'there were daily prepared no less than eighty-six tables groaning under five hundred dishes at each meal, not to speak of bread, beer and wine. This prodigious plenty in the King's Court caused amazement to foreigners and was much honour for the Kingdom'. It was not to last. When Cromwell sent his Commissioners to evaluate Tutbury, they estimated that the 140 horses stabled there were worth £1,982. And though the Great Protector banned horse-racing and the Royal Studs fell away somewhat, Cromwell was well aware of the huge need to re-establish horse-breeding as a national pre-occupation. The carnage of the Civil War had decimated the equestrian population just as badly as the human one. When Charles II returned to England to assume the throne in 1660, he sent the Sergeant-at-Arms to seize Oliver Cromwell's seven horses.

Charles II simply picked up from where his grandfather left off. He attended Epsom in 1661 and was much influenced in many of his equestrian decisions by the Duke of Newcastle, then the foremost breeder in the country. The King established the New market Town Plate which was to run over the newly-built round course on the second Thursday in October, 'for ever'. It still remains the only race run at Newmarket devoid of the Jockey Club's jurisdiction, and the 'Rowley Mile' at Newmarket is still an acknowledged feature of the course. King Charles's favourite hack was called 'Old Rowley', and his mainly admiring subjects took the name up as their affectionate nickname for him. The diarist John Evelyn was not so generous: 'Jolly blades racing, dancing, feasting and revelling, more resembling a lux-

*Over the
sticks at
the Windsor
Show, 1999*

urious and abandoned rout, than a Christian Court', was his description of a visit he made to Newmarket. William III continued the importation of foreign stock into the Studs, but it would be Queen Anne who next embraced wholeheartedly the thrill of the race-course. It was she who established the Royal Racecourse at Ascot, bred a grey gelding called Pepper who won three races at York and even had a bay colt, Star, run and win a sweepstake of forty guineas, just a few short days before her death. 'New-market's glory rose, as Britain's fell,' sniffed Alexander Pope.

The first two George's were not enamoured of the Turf. George II's second son, however, William, Duke of Cumberland, would achieve remarkable success, when, after the humiliation of losing a battle to the French in 1757, he retired from public life to Windsor where he had been made Ranger of Windsor Great Park. He would spend the last eight years of his life continuing to build up the Thoroughbreds at the Windsor Stud. Cumberland had begun his involvement with the Stud around 1750. In 1758 Herod was born. Twenty-two years later, when the horse died, Herod's stock had won over £200,000 in stakes. The other great stallion bred by Cumberland was Eclipse. According to Michael Oswald, manager of the Royal Studs and racing manager to both The Queen and the Queen Mother, in his Foreword for *Royal Thoroughbreds* by Arthur Fitzgerald: '... some 95 per cent of all Thoroughbreds descend in the male line from Eclipse and a high proportion of the remainder from Herod'. Cumberland, sometimes only now rather unfairly remembered as 'The Butcher of Culloden', had a huge influence, perhaps the most important, on the development of the Thoroughbred of any breeder in the country.

His nephew, Henry Frederick, younger brother of George III was also created Duke of Cumberland and he continued his uncle's passion. Between 1767 and 1781 he bred twenty-six winners of ninety-four races. Somewhat given to debauchery, Cumberland was much adored by his nephew, the Prince of Wales. When Eclipse's foal, Annette, sold by the Prince of Wales to pay his debts, won the Oaks in 1787, it was the very first time a member of the Royal Family had bred a Classic winner.

The financial problems which dogged him for most of his troubled days ensured that his enemies (and his creditors) caused him to sell 'by AUCTION by Messrs Tattershalls, near Hyde Park Turnpike ... the stud of His Royal Highness The Prince of Wales' twice. It did not stop him from beginning again and still managing to court scandal. When his jockey was accused of mishandling a horse at Newmarket, the Prince not only continued to pay the man a salary, but he never returned to the racecourse again. When he finally became King, the Newmarket stewards wrote him: '...we humbly request that Your Royal Highness will bury in oblivion any past unfortunate Occurences at Newmarket and that You will again be pleased to honor us there with your Countenance and Support'. King George IV never replied. His racing zeal continued however, and his patronage ensured that Lewes, set across the downs at Brighton, would rival Ascot and Newmarket in the racing and social calendar. Even on his deathbed, the King sent instruction that the racing results from Ascot be immediately brought by special messenger, race by race. Despite all his energies to rebuild the stud at Hampton Court, he would never win the Gold Cup.

His brother, William IV, had no interest in much else than the navy. His wife, Queen Adelaide, took her sewing with her when she attended Ascot. When the King was asked which of the royal horses should run in the Goodwood Cup in 1830, he announced, 'Let the whole squadron sail!' However, during William's reign, the Royal Studs bred Pocahontas, an exceptional broodmare who raised Stockwell, the champion sire for seven years between 1860 and 1873. The King's will did allow the Studs to be sold and since the Prime Minister, Lord Melbourne, had as little regard for the Turf as his late King, the petition not to sell from the Jockey Club had little affect. An editorial in *The Sporting Magazine* of September, 1837, described the Royal Studs as 'superior to any other in the world.' They were still sold.

As with her ancestor, Henry VIII, it was the need to be recognized as a properly equipped monarch that persuaded Queen Victoria to let her consort, Prince Albert, re-establish the Royal Studs at Hampton Court in 1849. As with his creation of a modern working farm at Windsor or designing a fine new residence on the Isle of Wight, Prince Albert's keenness was more to utilize his awareness of the latest methods of animal management or architectural materials, rather than a love of racing. It was considered only proper that the monarch of the greatest Empire in the world should own better horses than her European cousins. Although Queen Victoria did once get so excited, watching the New Stakes Race at Ascot in 1854, she broke a pane of glass as her head struck against it. Both Victoria and Albert attended Ascot each Tuesday and Thursday until Albert's death in 1861. Victoria never set foot on a race-course again. Her son and heir, the Prince of Wales, would take a rather different approach.

'I am always most anxious,' wrote Edward, the Prince of Wales, to his mother in 1870, 'to meet your wishes, dear Mama, in every respect, and always regret if we are not quite *d'accord* – but I am past twenty-eight and have some considerable knowledge of the world.' Edward had already bought Sandringham in 1864, the year he was elected to the Jockey Club. 'But I must bear it with philosophy,' he wrote, 'as I know what the glorious uncertainties of the Turf are.' In 1886 he created his own Stud at Sandringham, relying on the considerable expertise and traditions of the other Royal Studs.

We know from a reply to an Austrian breeder who wrote to enquire in 1887 that Hampton utilized twenty-six paddocks and thirty foals were born, on average, each year. Colonel Maude managed the Stud with the Stud Groom, nine helpers and temporary staff, now and then, at certain busy times of the year. In 1894, when Hampton was finally closed, in its forty-five years existence, it had bred the winner of every classic race; 349 horses who between them won 1,503 races. It had been one of the most successful studs in England.

For Edward, Prince of Wales, racing ownership was to become his most favoured sport and pleasure. By the time he became King in 1901, he had already won the Derby in 1896, and when his colt, Minoru, won the classic race again, by a short head, in 1909, the huge crowd immediately burst into a rousing rendition of 'God Save the King'! It was the first time that the Derby had been won by a reigning monarch. By 1904, Edward would head the list of winning owners, having won stakes worth £25,586. He had even defended racing in a letter to *The Times*, published at the time of the infamous 'Baccarat' scandal when a group of somewhat dissolute toffs were caught gambling illegally with a pack of marked cards, provided by, it was said, the Prince of Wales himself. Attacking the sins of gambling, his letter went on to describe racing as 'manly' and saw 'no reason why it should be looked upon as a gambling transaction'.

In 1895, the Prince's trainer, Lord Marcus Beresford wrote to tell him, 'Well, this is the first time we shall ever have a chance of a Derby horse...'. Persimmon went on to win the Derby the following year. When he was retired to stud, Persimmon achieved the coveted status of Champion Sire four times and when, due to an accident, the horse was put down in 1908, the King commissioned a statue of the famous horse which still stands at the entrance to the Royal Stud at Sandringham. King Edward VII achieved great success; he won the Derby three times, the Triple Crown with Diamond Jubilee in 1900, and the Grand National with Ambush the same year. On the King's death, his son, George V , would inherit eighteen broodmares at Sandringham and fourteen horses in training at Newmarket.

King George V loved being at Sandringham. He was a first-class shot, enjoyed shooting parties and within the grounds and estate of his own father's creation, he could become the true countryman that he so clearly liked to be. The new King even kept the tradition established by King Edward of putting the clocks at Sandringham half-an-hour ahead of the time everywhere else in the country. 'Sandringham Time' made ironic play of Queen Alexandra's habitual ability to always be late, but it also provided the King with more time out shooting. King George 'loved a day's racing', reported his horse-trainer, 'and no owner was keener or took a greater interest in his horses than he did'. That he also loved to walk his favourite granddaughter around the stables may begin to explain The Queen's exceptional knowledge of horses. For when her father finally became King and was visiting the Studs with his eldest daughter, it is reported that it was Princess Elizabeth who pointed out to her father the 2,000 Guineas winner, Big Game. According to Arthur Fitzgerald's book, *Royal Thoroughbreds*, the Princess later admitted to not washing her hands for some time, it had been such a privilege to touch so fine a colt. Not that her father was not an accomplished horse rider. He certainly adored hunting, and he and his wife were both extraordinarily fond of country pursuits. In this respect, as perhaps in many others, the Duke and Duchess of York were very different from the Prince of Wales and Wallis Simpson, the woman he choose, finally, to sacrifice his throne for. Edward also loved hunting. Both he and his brother Bertie (he took the name George on succeeding to the Throne after Edward's abdication) were keen horse riders. Edward actually won a race at the Household Brigade meeting at Hawthorn Hill and was watched doing it by his parents. He loved riding in point-to-point races and steeplechases, and though his younger brother was not so keen on the more abrasive types of racing, Bertie was considered, it seems, to have been the better rider of the two royal brothers. The traumatic shock waves caused by the Abdication crisis even impinged on the Royal Studs. Edward, it appears, had never liked Sandringham. On his accession, he announced his decision to sell the estate. All twenty broodmares were moved to Hampton Court, but as the crisis developed and Edward did choose to leave the Throne, the new King George was forced to buy Sandringham back from his eldest brother, when it became clear that the ex-king faced a lifetime's exile.

'I shall,' wrote the new King to his trainer, 'certainly take a great interest in Racing, but of course at the moment I know nothing about breeding or anything else. So you must teach me.' Whilst Duke of York, The Queen's father had often taken his two daughters out riding with him in Windsor Great Park, where the family lived when not in London. And though more serious teaching would follow under the guidance of Horace Smith, there can be little doubt that both Princess Elizabeth and her sister, Princess Margaret, encountered a great many of their formative equestrian experiences in the company of their father. It was their mother, however, who would become, perhaps, the most famous horse owner of them all.

Penelope Mortimer's sprightly biography of the Queen Mother tells an interesting anecdote. 'When one of her horses died, the Exchange Telegraph's broadcast service to the nation's betting shops was interrupted by the solemn announcement. One racing correspondent was foolish enough to suggest that the punters resented this - millions of pounds after all, could have been lost. He was as good as lynched.' Mrs Mortimer quotes from Frank Keating, writing in the *Guardian* in 1984: 'If there is a shorter cut to a bloody nose in Tattershall's than to criticize the Queen Mum in anyway, I do not know it.' Besides showing how much one newspaper can change in a quarter of a century, the story is illustrative of the very special affection which was evident from all sections of the British public when it came to the Queen Mother and her horses.

With well over four hundred winners, three in the same day in June 1961, a racing news ticker installed in Clarence House to help her with her studies, and a fair share of epic drama – the collapse of Devon Loch fifty yards from the finish (ridden by Dick Francis) in the Grand National when the horse had the race at his mercy, is just one of them – did ensure that the Queen Mother's racing achievements would become the stuff of legend. It was said that she intended to win the 2004 Cheltenham Gold Cup and it is, perhaps, most fitting, that one of her very last engagements, just ten days before her passing, would be her attendance at a private racing party near Windsor.

Queen Elizabeth took special delight in encouraging the young at the Windsor Show

According to most racing journalists who contributed to the enormous number of affectionate tributes which appeared in the Press over the Easter holidays of 2002, the Queen Mother had a huge influence in the revival of racing over hurdles and fences. Although Edward VII had achieved a Grand National winner, the Royal Family's racing interests since then had almost exclusively been concerned with the flat. In 1949, Lord Mildmay was invited to stay at Windsor Castle to attend the Royal Ascot meeting. Anthony Mildmay had been the most successful amateur rider in all the five National Hunt seasons since the end of the Second World War. His passion for the thrills of jumping, a sport described by Will Ogilvy as 'a game made by the Gods for brave men's playing', communicated itself to mother and daughter and both bought the horse Monaveen, through Mildmay's great friend Peter Cazalet. Though no horses would be shared again, Monaveen's first two wins at Fontwell Park and Hurst Park, kindled a passion in the Queen Mother for National Hunt racing. Sir Michael Oswald, who would manage the Royal Stud, maintained

More prize giving, Windsor, 1946

the Queen Mother preferred 'steeplechasing because it's not commercialised and arguably involves more colourful people. They are a bit more fun. In those days it was a smaller world, and a very nice one.'

In his book *Fit for a Queen* by the former jockey Richard Pitman, the Queen Mother put her passion quite simply. 'I've always wanted to have a horse for steeple-chasing, of course The Queen is very keen on the flat. So I thought I'd have one horse and see, it was no surprise when I got hooked, absolutely. I've had fun ever since.' And fun she certainly had. One anecdote must suffice, again from Pitman's entertaining book. One of her trainers, Nicky Henderson, was sitting next to the Queen Mother at a Savoy luncheon the day she had a horse running in the 3.10 race at Fontwell Park. 'She quietly ventured, 'Do you think we will be able to slip away in time to watch the horse? If you can follow me".' They left the table at 2.55pm and Henderson jumped a cab and ordered it to race behind the royal Rolls Royce as the Queen Mother sped around Eros and down into the Mall. They made Clarence House in time to watch the race on SISS, the satellite system that televises up to five race meetings a day. 'I only hope,' said Mr Henderson, 'that I can move as smart-ly when I reach the age of 94'.

The Queen would inherit twenty mares from her father and she would show that the years of asking her father's trainers about Thoroughbred bloodlines, stable man-agement and breeding stood her in good stead. After the court came out of its three month mourning in May 1952, Stream of Light won the Lancashire Oaks race. It was the first time The Queen's racing colours would be seen – purple, scarlet sleeves, gold tassel and a black velvet hat with another gold tassel.

That The Queen takes a highly active and informed interest in her racing con-cerns is borne out by comparing how she deals with racing matters, as opposed to some of the other complex choices she must make, such as that of worthy poets. She always picks her own jockeys, for example. Four days after her coronation, her chest-nut colt, Aureole, on whom great hopes had been placed came second in the Derby. Her two racing managers were in some disagreement about changing jockeys. She took the decision. The Order of Merit is an honour 'in The Queen's gift'. She can do with it what she likes. Yet Harold Nicholson tells in his journals of the terrible time he suffered fretting, because on being asked by The Queen's Deputy Secretary to whom The Queen might choose to represent the best of England's poets, Nicholson had rather rubbished the suggestion of Edith Sitwell.

Aureole did eventually repay all that attention. In 1954, when The Queen was the season's top owner in terms of stake money, the horse unseated his rider at Epsom. Calling the horse back, the jockey remounted and won, three-quarters of a length ahead of the rest. There is eye-witness corroboration that The Queen almost ran to greet the horse into the winner's enclosure. And Aureole continued to please, siring the Derby winner, St Paddy. Like her mother, two copies of *Sporting Life* were deliv-ered to her daily and both mother and daughter kept very close contact. The widow of one of the greatest royal trainers, Peter Cazalet, tells a touching story of how the Queen Mother was watching a race, which she won, on the television at Clarence

House. The phone rang immediately. The Queen Mother told Cazalet that that would be The Queen telling her, 'Well done', and it was.

The Queen was allowed to read her father's personal racing reports when her clear passion for the Turf became clear. Rising Light was to become an especial favourite of both father and daughter, for it was the very first horse to win wearing the King's own racing colours; it was the Burghfield Stakes, at Ascot in 1945, and both George VI and Princess Elizabeth were there to welcome the winner into the enclosure. They had attended Ascot just hours after the King had lunched President Truman at Windsor. The American President informed his host that atomic bombs would shortly be dropped on Japan.

The Queen leads Lester Piggott on her horse Carrozza after winning the Oaks in June 1957

Queen Elizabeth II watching Anbosson after winning the St James's Stakes at Epsom, May 1963

The King had appointed Captain Charles Moore as manager of the Royal Stud, and Princess Elizabeth was to learn an enormous amount of horse and racing wisdom from talking with him. Captain Moore would manage the Royal Stud for twenty-three years, before supervising the handing over of it over to his deputy, Brigadier A.D.R. Wingfield in 1960. By then The Queen had already been well-recognized, within the racing world, as a very fine judge of horses.

She would give up racing under National Hunt Rules in 1952, the same year as she would achieve her very first winner, Choir-Boy, at Newmarket in May, and also announce her wish to continue with the Royal Stud, under the guidance of Captain Boyd-Rochfort. Two years later, in 1954, the victories of Aureole would contribute, amongst others, to The Queen becoming the leading owner and the Captain, the leading trainer, of that year. According to Arthur Fitzgerald, Aureole was 'the most influential stallion to stand at the Royal Stud since Persimmon'. The horse was the leading sire of winners in 1960 and 1961 and was second in 1965. Aureole would die in 1974, just two years before his great-grandson won the Derby.

In 1969 Lord Porchester became racing manager to The Queen, a grandson of the 5th Earl of Carnarvon (of Tutankhamun fame), and a racing man all his life. Michael Oswald became stud manager to The Queen, taking over from Major Richard Shelley, who had been manager since Brigadier Wingfield's retirement in 1963. Michael Oswald would also become racing manager to the Queen Mother. The Queen now used two trainers, in the main, Ian Balding at Kingslere, and Dick Hern at West Ilsley, which meant she could spend more time watching her horses perform as both training establishments were nearer to London than Sandringham.

Six of the foals bred by The Queen in 1955 would become winners, but 1959 would become the worst year at the Royal Stud since 1944. Aureole's son, Apprentice, won the Goodwood Cup in 1964 (The Queen had asked the Royal Military College at Sandhurst to bring the Sovereign's parade forward by fifteen minutes so she could get to Goodwood in time to see it); in 1967, seven foals trained by Ian Balding and Major Hern became winners, which compensated somewhat for a poor showing of good foals in 1964 and 1965. Perhaps the greatest disappointment, however, was the tragic end of Magna Carta, who won the Doncaster Cup in 1970. A year later this potential winner of the elusive Ascot Gold Cup broke his jaw on a

The Queen with Magna Carta, after winning the Ascot Stakes, June 1970

hay-net; an accident which led The Queen to ban them from her horses' boxes, when in transit, ever since.

It was Lord Porchester who suggested mating Highlight with Queen's Hussar and the resulting bay filly was named Highclere by The Queen. In the 1973 1,000 Guineas at Newmarket, after a photo-finish, Highclere became the first Classic winner bred by the Queen to be greeted by Her Majesty in the unsaddling enclosure. (Pall Mall, who won the 2000 Guineas at Kempton in 1958 had been the first, but The Queen had been unwell and Princess Anne had welcomed the winner back.) Highclere went on to win the Prix de Diane at Chantilly and become the first filly to win that double. 'I was kissed by several ladies I had never met before, and by some Frenchmen as well', remembered Michael Oswald, and the jockey, Joe Mercer, remembers the dinner at Windsor Castle the evening of the French victory as 'the greatest day in our lives'.

In 1972, in part due to the political situation in Ireland, The Queen's broodmares began to go to Kentucky, and The Queen still keeps horses there, although she has joined in the use of syndicated stallions since 1969. She would win the Oaks with Dunfermline in 1977, and in 1982 sold her broodmare, Height of Fashion, for over a million pounds. Her third foal, Nashwan, would win the 2,000 Guineas, the Derby, the Eclipse Stakes and the King George VI and Queen Elizabeth Diamond Stakes. No colt had ever won these four races in one year (1989). But despite these spectacular successes during her first decade, from 1968 till 1990, The Queen had only five wins in British racing. The recent death of Lord Porchester must have been a desperate blow both for The Queen and indeed all the staff who attend her and her horses.

Despite a lean few racing years, her enthusiasm remains. She still names all her horses and displays a ready wit with their lineage. 'Mister Glum by Ron's Victory out of Australian Fair' pays homage to the very popular radio show of the 1950s, *Take It From Here* and 'Feel Free by Generous out of As You Desire Me' will be left to the reader to consider. And it's well documented that the daily racing press is still studied over the royal breakfast. The Queen, however, has equestrian interests which may more than compensate for her rather bleak racing form of late and we next will look at one of the most delightful, The Royal Windsor Royal Horse Show.

·Chapter Four·

THE ROYAL WINDSOR HORSE SHOW

On June 2nd 1944, the *Horse and Hound* carried the following:

'Windsor Horse Show, held in the Home Park, was honoured by the presence of the King and Queen; their Majesties spent some four hours watching the competitions. This was the first show held by the recently formed Royal Windsor Horse Show Club, and it had the enormous advantage of having the King as patron for the show.

'The afternoon was all the more memorable because Princess Elizabeth and Princess Margaret were successful in two of the classes. At the close Major Faudel-Phillips, who had conducted a running commentary throughout the day, said he was convinced that the show was likely to be one of the great shows of England, and that it was running Richmond very close.'

This report was of the second Windsor Horse Show. The first one was announced as a 'Horse Show, Gymkhana and Dog Show'. It had been organized, under the auspices of the town's Entertainment Committee, as part of the 'Wings for Victory Week' activities on Wednesday, May 26th 1943, 'commencing at 1.45pm'. The Silver Challenge Cup was supplied by the Alexander Clark Company of Leadenhall Street, EC3, who also took the main advertisement on the front page of the programme (costing sixpence) with the slogan: 'It's the Royal Borough So make it Thorough!' And thorough the hundred-odd participants had to be. Petrol rationing prohibited most entrants from transporting their horses by road. They cheerfully hacked their way there, however, some from as far as thirty miles away. Valerie Millwood 'went to the very first Windsor. We took the horses on the train from Goring-on-Thames and we rode

The Royal Windsor Horse Show

The two Princesses win first prize at Windsor in 1944

from the station through the town. We all had to have headcollars in case there was an air raid.'

Remembering its early days, fifty years later, the co-founder and then still chairman of the Royal Windsor Horse Show, Geoffrey Cross, claimed it was all due to food poisoning. Catching typhoid after eating some suspect oysters, the 25-year-old bombardier was reluctantly invalided out of the Army and keen to help the war effort. His grandfather had helped to found the Hawthorn Hill pony racing track (where Edward VIII, when Prince of Wales had rode), so horses were in the blood. His friend, Count Robert Orssich, who had moved near to Windsor, had organized many horse shows around Europe before the outbreak of the war. It was their enthusiasm and talents which got the very first show up and running.

King George VI gave permission to hold the event at Windsor Castle; the show raised £2,700, cost £1,200 to put on and a very decent contribution to the 'Wings for Victory' appeal was raised, in what were very difficult days indeed. Not that all went smoothly, as Geoffrey Cross remembered: 'I realised at the first show, that the garden chairs under the awning, the sort one would expect to see at weddings ... were facing away from Windsor Castle, the finest backdrop in the world. There was an unpleasant fight in the dog show, a lurcher stole a chicken from the caterer's tent, which in those times was a big loss because of strict rationing, and none of it, it turned out, conformed with Kennel Club rules. I vowed there would be no dogs there again.'

In November that year the Royal Windsor Horse Show Club was founded and King George VI accepted an invitation to become the Show's patron, a position his daughter still retains. There were three hundred founder members. Lord Wigram, who had been patron of the 1943 show, became the first life vice-president, the Duke of Beaufort became president and the very first Royal Windsor Horse Show was held on May 27th, 1944. This time the awnings and chairs faced the right way, directly across from the magnificent edifice of the Castle built high up on the ramparts looking over the Windsor Home Park.

Both the King and Queen attended, and the fact that the King was seen in public not dressed in a military uniform – the first time since war had been declared – was in some ways, a symbol of the close, clearly affectionate, connection the Show would always maintain with its Royal patrons. Other members of the Royal Family attended and Princesses Elizabeth and Margaret competed, for the very first time in public. Besides being the passenger to her sister, as Princess Elizabeth drove Hans to First Prize in the Single Private Driving Class, Princess Margaret held the 'ribbons' of Gypsy in the utility driving class, and was presented with her cup by her father.

Over eight thousand people came to watch the show. The band of the Royal Horse Guards, The Blues, contributed a stirring musical accompaniment – a tradition which still remains – and two Red Cross nurses were put up for the night at the Castle, at the invitation of the King. Thumbing a lift, as transport was still an acute problem, the two nurses hitched a ride with none other than the Duke of Beaufort, on his way to the show ground. Reporting the story to the King and Queen, the Duke mentioned that Geoffrey Cross had told him the nurses were also having trouble finding a place to stay. 'I think', said King George VI, 'we can probably find a spare room at the Castle'. And that's exactly where they stayed.

What had started in such a small way with an announcement in the May 21st, 1943 issue of the *Horse and Hound* ('Windsor Wings for Victory Week. Horse show, gymkhana and dog show to be held in the Home Park, Windsor Castle. £10 first prize open jumping.') would become the largest outdoor horse show in Britain, and the last surviving classic horse show, as the 'Royal International' changed and the 'Richmond Royal' closed. 'It stands alone,' wrote Alan Smith in his 1976 account, *The Royal Windsor Horse Show*, 'in equestrian elegance'.

By 1946, the Show lasted over two days with an impressive 720 entries. The following year it lasted three days as the Committee felt it was necessary 'to devote more time to the individual classes, and also to include some new ones'. One of which would be an 'International Trial Jumping Competition', partly in preparation for the 1948 Olympics (which were held in London) but also an indication of the growing enthusiasm amongst both spectators and participants for Show Jumping. Eighteen thousand people would attend the Show in 1948, no doubt some attracted, by the very first time the musical ride of the Household Cavalry was performed by a combined contingent of the Life Guards and the Royal Horse Guards, The Blues. Besides the thrill of witnessing military history, it was also the first time the ride had been performed by either regiment since 1939.

Overleaf: Sporting Life *report the 1969 show*

The two Princesses with Lord Beaufort, Windsor 1946

Royal Windsor

HORSE SHOW

HOME PARK, WINDSOR

8th, 9th, 10th & 11th
MAY, 1969

FLOODLIT EVENING SESSIONS

MUSICAL RIDE
by
**THE ROYAL CANADIAN
MOUNTED POLICE**

Saturday Evening
MUSICAL DRIVE BY
THE KING'S TROOP R.H.A.

TICKETS FROM

Alfred Hays Ltd., Trafalgar Square, 4/5 Charing Cross, S.W. ;
and 74 Cornhill, E.C.3

Keith Prowse & Co., Ltd. 90 New Bond Street, London, W.1

Also Principal Ticket Agencies throughout the Country
or direct from

Tufnell & Partners, Estate Agents, 2 Sheet Street, Windsor
(Tel.: Windsor 60370)

A splendid mixture of colour, pageantry

"Everywhere there are people strolling, chatting, laughing and, above all, watching the action in the ring or on the outside course. Even this watching has a quality of its own. It may be the appreciative attention given good horses in competition; again it's the rapt gaze of a horse-smitten youngster, or it's the awed, breath-holding attention of an owner watching his horse in action, perhaps it's the analytical scrutiny of the professional calculating the present and future chances for his horses and himself.

"Seeing it all, you realise that there's nothing quite like it anywhere else."

THE above passage is taken from the catalogue of one of the best-known horse shows and country fairs in the United States.

But it might equally well be applied to the Royal Windsor Horse Show, which opens in the Home Park at Windsor Castle on Thursday, May 8, under the sponsorship of the David Brown Companies, and continues for four days.

Windsor is the first of the classic shows, a splendid mixture of pageantry and prowess; and, now that its twin sister at Richmond has fallen by the wayside, it occupies a unique position in the calendar as London's premier national show.

A major attraction this year will be the performances given by the Royal Canadian Mounted Police, whose celebrated musical ride was last seen in this country in 1957.

Mounted on their black horses and wearing the traditional dress of Stetson hat, scarlet tunic, blue breeches, long boots, spurs, brown gauntlets and full Sam Browne equipment, the "Mounties" can be relied upon to present a display at once colourful and polished.

Foremost among our own home-bred displays, I would put the musical drive by the King's Troop of the Royal Horse Artillery, and the nine-horse coaching marathon.

By MICHAEL WILLIAMS

The drive consists of four officers and 70 N.C.Os and men in full-dress uniform with their gun carriages; and the marathon of eight magnificent vehicles (including a coach and four driven by the Queen, each carrying a complement of not less than six people.

Competitive event

The coaching marathon is a competitive event, and, in making the awards, the judges take into account the quality of the horses and their condition after a nine-mile drive, and the smartness of the turn-out.

The coaches are required to undertake a preliminary drive before assembling in the ring for the final judging, and I was amused to note that the regulations permit the vehicles to pass each other on the road "provided it is done in a proper coachman-like manner."

This, I understand, precludes galloping, which is perhaps just as well on our modern roads; and clearly bumping and boring also comes into a coach-man-like category for the purpose of this very gentlemanly marathon, which would undoubtedly cause John Mytton to turn in that restless grave of his.

Satisfactory entry

The entries for the Windsor Show are a little down on last year's record of 1,637, but they are within 50 of it, which is still very satisfactory, especially as the near-clash with the international show in Barcelona (May 11-18) has necessarily meant fewer entries from some of the big jumping stables.

But Harvey Smith, Alan Oliver, Alison Westwood, Judy Crago, Jean Goodwin, John Kidd and Ted and Elizabeth Edgar are among those with entries in the jumping classes; and it will be interesting to see Derek Kent riding Havana Royal, the horse with which Althea Roger Smith did so well.

Kent's star pupil, Michael Saull Hall, is expected to ride his pony Pablo in the junior jumping championship.

The show classes are always exciting, and invariably bring out the top performers in this field.

One of these, Lady Teller, the five-year-old show on whom David Tatlow won the hack championship at the Royal International Horse Show and the Horse of the Year Show last year, is due to make her first appearance of the season at Newark today. Her next will be at Windsor.

Also bound for Windsor are two more of the Tatlow horses, State Visit, the heavyweight hunter on whom he won the hunter championship at the Horse of the Year Show; and Park Royal, an iron-grey four-year-old by an American sire High Powers out of a Hyperion mare.

Park Royal, who is owned by Mr. Denis Redfern, of Coxtorni Radings, will be competing in the novice hack class.

David Tatlow had 119 wins in show classes last season, when he engaged in some memorable duels with Donald Green, another great showman, who got the better of him in the hunter championship at the Royal International Horse Show on Sporting Rights.

The week's highlights

Tatlow, on State Visit, and Owen, on Sporting Rights, in the hunter championship at Windsor should certainly be one of the highlights of next week's show.

The events in the main ring commence on Thursday, May 8, at 9.15 a.m. with a class for novice hunters, followed by lightweights, middleweights and heavyweights and culminating, at 4.15 p.m., in the hunter championship, for which ladies' hunters (to be ridden side-saddle) are also eligible.

But before the hunter championship comes the first of the jumping competitions in the main arena, a contest for Grade "B" horses timed to start at 2.30 p.m.

The three highest-placed

horses in this event, together with those in the three Grade "C" competitions, which take place during the morning in the secondary ring, will qualify to compete in the Walwyn Novice Jumping Championship to be decided immediately after the hunter championship at 4.30 p.m.

The other classes on the first afternoon include hackney pairs and tandems, Household Cavalry remounts, trade and agricultural light turnouts and a class for working hunters.

Finally, at 7.05 p.m., there is a tent pegging competition, with lances, for teams of four.

The second day opens with hack classes, and the afternoon events include the first of the Grade "A" jumping competitions (at 2.15 p.m.) and the final judging of the coaching marathon (4.0 p.m.).

There is also a floodlit evening session, which starts at 6.0 p.m. with the preliminary stages of the Aston Martin Lagonda Ladies' Jumping Championship, the winner of which qualifies for the Queen Elizabeth II Cup at the Royal International Horse Show.

The jump-off for the ladies jumping championship is at 9.15 p.m. and is preceded by the hack championship; and at 10.10 p.m. the Royal Canadian Mounted Police give the first of their musical rides.

Children's pony day

On the Saturday, when the children's ponies come into their own with five classes and a championship, there are two services team jumping competitions, one in the morning and one in the afternoon, and a speed jumping contest.

The afternoon performance on this day concludes with the second appearance of the Royal Canadian Mounted Police (5.0 p.m.), who make their third and final appearance at the floodlit evening session at 9.45 p.m.

They are followed at 10.15 p.m. by the King's Troop, Royal Horse Artillery, with their musical drive.

The big competitive event at this evening session is the David Brown Tractors' Supreme Jumping Championship, timed for 8.45 p.m.

This is confined to the five highest placed horses in the Grade "A" contest earlier in the evening and the ladies' championship on the previous day.

On Sunday, May 11, the last day of the show, the single performance in the afternoon begins at 2.0 p.m. with a preliminary qualifying competition for the Royal Windsor Junior Jumping Championship, the final stages of which are due to start at 4.0 p.m.

The other major jumping event, the David Brown St. George of England Jumping Competition, for Grade "A" horses, incorporates the Berkshire Area International Trial.

Qualifier for Wembley

The winner of this earns automatic qualification for either the King George V Gold Cup or the Queen Elizabeth II Cup at Wembley in July.

Also on this last afternoon are three more leisurely, but none the less delightful events.

The first is a parade of donkeys organised in conjunction with the Donkey Show Society. Then comes a Meet of the British Driving Society, in which about 100 vehicles are expected to take part.

This is followed by a competition for teams of three from the riding clubs.

SHOW JUMPING

IS betting on show-jumping going to change the pattern of the shows? That is the question which many people will have been asking before the competition starts. There may well be many people at the Sussex showground who can look forward to a flutter when the Men's European Show Jumping Championship is staged there on July 17-20, and the British Jumping Derby is featured during the further international show on August 14-17.

But it is one to which no positive answer can yet be given, writes **Michael Williams**.

Certainly the venture appears to have been successful, and in fact the London layers will be represented at the Royal Windsor. Ladbrokes, at Hickstead

Prospective visitors to the Sussex showground can look forward to a flutter when the Men's European Show Jumping Championship is staged there on July 17-20, and the British Jumping Derby is featured during the further international show on August 14-17.

In between these two shows comes the Royal International Horse Show at Wembley on July 22-27, to which teams from Italy, France, Germany, Switzerland, Ireland and Sweden have been invited.

I would like to think that Ladbrokes will be making a book on major events there, but have my doubts.

One show at which a repre-

sentative of the firm would be welcome is the Prince Beckett Jumping Show, in aid of the Slade Memorial Gymkhana. The Sports Movement of the Patients on August 12.

This show, which serves such a splendid cause, and at which the late Lionel Vick was treasurer for many years, features a National Hunt Jockeys' Jumping Competition, which is surely a thoroughly well to do dream for a few.

The horse show season is just beginning to get into its stride, and by the time the Royal Windsor comes along it will be building up to a crescendo.

In June there is the B.S.J.A. National Ladies' Championships at the South of England Show at Ardingly; in the July

HORSE SHOWS

IN THE HOME PARK

Harvey Smith, on O'Malley, takes a fence.

The Run for the Roses on Churchill Downs

By JOE HIRSCH

TODAY all roads in Eastern America lead to Louisville and the 95th Kentucky Derby

The Run for the Roses appears one of the most intriguing American classics in years and possibly the best Kentucky Derby since 1957, when Calumet Farm's Iron Liege upset an all-star field including Gallant Man, Round Table and Bold Ruler.

The favourite is Frank McMahon's underrated Majestic Prince, a chestnut colt by Raise A Native out of Gay Hostess, by Royal Charger, who has won his seven starts, including the 91 Santa Anita Derby.

Record bid

Bill Hartack, seeking to equal Eddie Arcaro's record of five Kentucky Derby triumphs, has the mount on Majestic Prince, who is trained by Johnny Longden.

Winner of more than 6,600 races as a rider, Longden estimates Majestic Prince to be the equal of Count Fleet, whom

he rode to win the Triple Crown in 1943

Kentuckians got their first glimpse of Majestic Prince in the seven-furlong Stepping Stone Purse on opening day at Churchill Downs.

Majestic Prince won by six lengths and his time of 1:21.6 almost equalled the track record, though he was never urged at any time and won under a double hold.

The other major contenders for the Kentucky Derby are:

Top Knight, by Vertex, out of Rap-Tan, by Summer Tan, owned by the Estate of Steven B. Wilson, trained by Ray Metcalf, and ridden by Manuel Ycaza

Top Knight won the nine-furlong Flamingo Stakes and Florida Derby in Miami this winter and is a tough, talented competitor in good hands.

Arts and Letters, by Ribot out of All Beautiful, by Battle-

field owned by Paul Mellon, trained by Elliot Burch and ridden by Bill Shoemaker

Arts and Letters finished second to Top Knight in the Flamingo and Florida Derby but won the nine-furlong Blue Grass Stakes at Keeneland last week by 15 lengths in a brilliant tour de force. He has speed and class.

Dike, by Herbager out of Delta by Nasrullah, owned by A. B. Hancock, trained by Lauren Laurin and ridden by Jorge Velazquez.

Dike won the nine-furlong Wood Memorial as if he is just coming to hand. He is a nice run horse with a strong closing punch and is superbly bred. Delta has been voted America's champion broodmare of the year.

First time

One of the highlights of the Kentucky Derby will be the visit of President Richard Nixon the first time in history that a President has gone racing while in office

Churchill Downs management has a large lawn on the roof, at an expenditure of £250,000 to hold the 250 persons who the Presidential party is safety and comfort

Accompanying the President will be the governors of 20 states, who have been meeting in nearby Lexington in a semi-annual conference

President Nixon attended last year's Kentucky Derby as a private citizen, and told Churchill Downs president Wathen Knebelkamp that he would return

Horsemen in New York have gone on strike seeking four days of additional racing in December for the benefit of hospitalization and pension plans for grooms exercise boys and others who work with horses

There has been a threat that the grooms and others would not remain unless the minimum wage raised, but Governor Nelson Rockefeller of New York says the action is disapproved and irresponsible, and adds that four days of racing for charity as the horsemen propose might be unforthcoming

Gulfstream Park in Miami concluded the 126-day Florida season a cash average of 10 races, a 4th grams 20,000 attended this card, which was unique in the United States

The Declared Appreciation Purse at eight and a half furlongs, was won by the five-year-old President, an Irish-bred horse by Proud Chieftain who races for the San Marco Stable.

Lou Smith, president of Rockingham Park in New Hampshire and one of the grand old men of American racing died at 81

Smith ran away from home as a boy, joined a circus, and tended elephants. In later years he sold rawhcoods, managed boxers, ran a pub, was in the cinema theatre business, worked for a wire company and held other jobs.

In 1906 he operated a small track in Tulsa, Oklahoma, and in succeeding years, managed racetracks in Montreal and in Texas.

He opened Rockingham in 1933, after personally pushing a pari-mutuel bill through the New Hampshire legislature Smith and his wife Lutza were noted for their charity work on behalf of crippled children.

BETTING IN BALANCE

National Championship at the Royal which has now found a permanent home at Kenilworth and in August, during the first three days of the Dublin Horse Show, the Ladies' European Championship, which is currently held by Anneli Drummond-Hay.

August is also the month of the H.S.J.A. Olympic Trial at the British Timken Show at Duston, Northampton, and of the two big Bank Holiday shows, the Greater London Show on Clapham Common and the Harlow (Essex) Town Show, which drew a crowd of 39,000 last year.

There are also innumerable smaller shows, including indoor ones, such as those which are held throughout the season at the Park Equestrian Centre at

Wing, Buckinghamshire, and the Warwickshire Equestrian Club, at Bubbeill Common, near Coventry.

These small shows, which far outnumber the bigger ones, are the very life-blood of the movement, and without them many of the best horses and riders that contribute so much to our enjoyment would never have had a start.

On September 4-7, W. D. & H. O. Wills, the Harkstead sponsors, present a four-day show which features the finals of the Junior Foxhunter Championship and the Young Riders Championship of Great Britain.

In October there is the show to end all shows, the Horse of the Year Show at the Empire Pool, Wembley, to which everything has been building up.

But this time there will be something to follow the Horse of the Year Show for on the nights of October 13, 14, 15, 17 and 16, the Empire Pool will be graced by the world-famous Spanish Riding School of Vienna, which is to give five complete performances of the art of classical riding as shown at the Hofreitschule in Vienna.

A sure sign of the ever-increasing popularity of equestrian activities is the amount of sponsorship they are enjoying from commercial firms and enterprises. The 1969 season is especially notable for three exciting new ventures in sponsorship over a wide field.

Show Jumping is among the sports which are to benefit from the B. Vat-69 Sportsmen of the Year contests that are being

introduced by William Sanderson and Son Ltd., the blenders of Scotch whiskies.

The Vat 69 Award will be made to the best British rider man or woman to achieve 23 wins on the basis of 3 points for each win between January 1 and December 31 in Grade "A" competitions, carrying a first prize of £50 or more and international competitions at home and abroad.

In the show ring there will be more money for the hunters, thanks to the generosity of the B. + I Shipping Line, who are making the hunter championship at the Horse of the Year Show the richest in the world, with £500 for the winner, £150 for the runner-up and £100 for the third.

But a great many other shows will reap some advantage from this, because 40 of them (including three in Ireland) have been invited to make their hunter classes qualifying events for the Wembley championship, and the B + I Line are giving each of them £10 in added prize money.

WEEK-END HORSE SHOWS
TODAY
[show listings]

TOMORROW
[show listings]

'In full dress uniform,' wrote Smith, 'the scarlet tunics and white plumes of the Life Guards, the blue tunics and scarlet plumes of the Royal Horse Guards, steel helmets gleaming like fire, cuirasses aloft, they wheeled their intricate display; the drummer with his solid silver drums, on his heroic piebald, a contrast to the black horses and the greys of the four trumpeters in their crimson and gold, the whole making a spectacle such as had not been seen in Britain for nearly a decade.'

1948 had another special connotation. It was the first time that radio broadcasting, directly from a equestrian event, took place. On the Saturday evening, on *Sports Review*, John Snagge reported to the nation on that day's happenings, and though he did rather over-emphasize the social aspects more than the sporting, it did mark the beginning of the huge involvement that the media, and especially television, would have in creating a mass interest in equestrian sports. For it was mostly farmers, soldiers and land-owners who had supported and taken part in horse events, before the 1960s. Television would create a whole new audience, as well as involving many city-dwellers in the thrill of watching, and maybe themselves taking up, equestrian activities. It would also prove to be significant that The Queen's love of horses would be passed on, with such impressive results, to her children.

Making the final adjustments

Princess Anne, the Princess Royal, in her book *Riding Through My Life*, remembers that '...we rode most Saturdays, but not on Sundays, because that was the groom's day off. The Home Park and the Great Park at Windsor were wonderful places to ride; plenty of space and with logs and fallen branches to jump.' At Sandringham: 'There were, and still are, 'rides', which had been planted or cleared for Queen Alexandra to be able to ride through the woods and all over the estate without getting her hat knocked off.' Besides becoming a European champion in the dangerous sport of Three-Day Eventing (on Doublet, owned and bred by The Queen), Princess Anne would also become the first British Royal ever picked for an Olympiad.

She distinguished herself on the Turf, as well, winning, amongst other races, the Queen Mother Diamond Stakes at Ascot in 1987 and the Queen Mother Cup at York in 1988, with Insular, owned and trained by Ian Balding, but bred by The

Queen. 'My limited experience,' wrote Princess Anne, 'of National Hunt Racing has given me as much satisfaction as anything I have ever done.'

Her father, Prince Philip, learned to ride at his school, Gordonstoun, but it was his uncle, Earl Mountbatten, who introduced Prince Philip to the thrills, and spills, of playing polo. The Prince captained the Windsor team until 1971, and his son, Prince Charles, would also develop a deep love for the game. Indeed, in 1970, during the same match watched by The Queen, both her husband and eldest son fell off their horses with startling force, causing Earl Mountbatten to caution a less enthusiastic approach to playing the game on the part of Prince Philip. It is reported that The Queen wrote to her husband's uncle: 'Wish me luck to see if I could stop him'.

Prince Philip would eventually become President of the Federation Equestre Internationale, the international ruling body for every equestrian sport apart from racing, but, perhaps more importantly for the Royal Windsor Horse Show, developed a taste for a new equestrian sport – Carriage Driving. Indeed the very first time that the new sport, based on the rules and conditions of the Three Day Event, was watched in England, was at the 1970 Royal Windsor Horse Show. Prince Philip would eventually be a member of the British team which won the Carriage Driving World Championships in 1976.

The Queen with Princess Anne, horse and corgis.

Princess Anne at Windsor, 1976

Princess Anne was only nine when she made her first prize presentation at Windsor, shaking the winner's hand and handing up a Hackney cup to Cynthia Haydon, and the Princess would make her competition debut there, in the Spillers Combined Training event in 1972. She finished fourth and fifth, riding Purple Star and Columbus, but would have to wait a year until winning the competition on her European champion, Doublet. In later years, the Princess Royal has encouraged representatives of Riding for the Disabled, of which she is President, to perform on the show ground, underlining her very real conviction that equestrian pursuits build confidence as well as allowing for huge enjoyment and exhilaration.

Prince Charles was taken to his first show, by his parents, in 1955. By the end of the 1970s he entered in a team of Welsh Guards, of which he is the Colonel, in the triathlon, and finished equal third. The *Horse and Hound* reported 'him smiling after the shooting phase, and still smiling when taking part in the jumping phase on his

Prince Charles plays polo at Windsor, 1976

sister's former novice eventer, Candlewick'. Prince Edward continued the Royal involvement entering the competition in 1989, and there would seem to be every indication that the next generation of the Royal Family are acquiring the same passion for horses and for the special quality of the Royal Windsor show to continue for what has, over the past fifty-odd years, become a unique relationship.

It is only fitting that the horse show in 'their back garden', has enjoyed such a long Royal patronage. Windsor, Royalty and horses seem criss-crossed together over generations, families, institutions and traditions. Horace Smith, who gave The Queen and her sister their first professional riding lessons was one of the original committee members for the Royal Windsor Horse Show. His father had been awarded a Royal Warrant of Appointment by Queen Victoria, the only horse dealer to ever be so honoured. And although the Royal Canadian Mounted

Police gave their first Musical Ride at Windsor in 1957, it was The Queen's great-grandfather, Edward VII, who had given the Mounties their royal prefix in 1904. It was in Queen Victoria's pony phaeton, built for her personal use at Windsor, that Princess Elizabeth, with Princess Margaret alongside her, won first prize at the very first Windsor show.

But for many people, especially now that the evening performances take place against the back-cloth of an illuminated Windsor Castle, the great highlight of the Royal Windsor Show is the 'drive' by the Royal Horse Artillery and the musical ride of the Household Cavalry. No celebration of The Queen and her horses would be complete without an account of one of the longest and most important relationships in this country's history; that of the Monarch to the nation's fighting forces.

Prince Phillip at Windsor, 1973

Opposite:
The carriages begin their progress towards the show ring, with Windsor Castle in the background

·CHAPTER FIVE·

THE SOLDIERS
OF THE QUEEN

When Edward I rode north from Carlisle in 1300 to subdue the rebellious Scots, an observer wrote:

> 'There were many rich caparisons embroidered on silks and satins; many a beautiful pennon fixed to a lance, many a banner displayed. The neighing of horses was heard from afar; the mountains and valleys were covered with pack-horses and waggons with provisions, tents and pavilions.'

The cavalry were always the elite of any army, and the medieval English cavalry usually had to be provided by the monarch, from amongst members of the royal household. The chronicler, Oderic Vitalis, maintained that Henry I's household included nearly 300 knights, providing more than enough personal protection. Indeed such was the allure and influence to be obtained from being a member of the King's entourage, that in his battles against the French, Henry I's household provided one of the three divisions constituting his total army. Though the struggle for power between monarch, nobility and parliament would wax and wane across the centuries, the monarch always played a pivotal role in the final allegiance of the army. The French chronicler Jean le Bel wrote of how impressive was the love of the English knights for their king, and the eagerness with which they were prepared to fight for him abroad.

And though the promise of land and pillage might also have been a factor, the symbolic bond that monarch and subject can achieve has no greater evidence than the impact Laurence Olivier's film of Shakespeare's *Henry V* had on the British nation in 1944. It was not without cause that Winston Churchill's wreath on the coffin of George VI read simply, 'For Valour'.

Of equal importance, perhaps, is the continuity and history of the various English, Scottish, Welsh and Irish regiments which would eventually constitute the British army. 'One way or another,' wrote General

Medieval Knight, Windsor 2000

Sir Ian Hamilton in 1921, 'the roots of tradition strike downwards'.

The Queen is Colonel-in-Chief to both Household Cavalry Regiments; the Life Guards and the Blues and Royals. The Life Guards are the senior Regiment of the Household Cavalry. Their uniform is scarlet with blue velvet facings. Their motto is *Honi Soit Qui Mal y Pense* (Evil be to him who Evil Thinks) and amongst their many nicknames are 'The Bangers', 'The Tin Bellies' and 'The Cheesemongers'. Their battle honours include Waterloo, South Africa 1899-1900, Passchendaele, Brussels, El Alamein and Italy 1944. Their Regimental Headquarters are the Horse Guards at Whitehall, a building they share with the Blues and Royals, with whom they also share the same motto.

The Blues and Royals wear a uniform which is blue with scarlet facings. The Regiment was formed by the amalgamation of two historic Regiments in 1969 – the Royal Horse Guards (The Blues) and the Royal Dragoons (1st Dragoons) – and their nicknames have, in the case of the Royal Horse Guards ('The Blues') become their official title, though the Royal Dragoons were known as 'The Birdcatchers', as well as 'The Royals'. The Royal Dragoons had their own motto, *Spectemur Agendo* (Let us be Judged by Our Deeds), and won as distinguished a list of battle honours, from Tangier in 1662 to Italy in 1943, as did the Blues, who won battle honours in all the major wars from the Napoleonic to World War II. The amalgamated regiment was given a battle honour for their gallantry during the Falkland campaign in 1982.

The Household Division is made up of seven Regiments; the Household Cavalry Regiments mentioned above, and five Regiments of Foot Guards (Grenadier, Coldstream, Scots, Irish and Welsh). The Grenadier Guards, as the senior regiment of the Foot Guards, are the infantry equivalent of the Household Cavalry. They were raised by an exiled Charles II in 1656 as the

Left:
*The drums
set the pace,
Windsor 1999*

Right:
*The King's
Troop prepare
for action,
Windsor 1999*

Royal Regiment of Guards and merged, after the King's restoration, with another regiment, becoming in 1685, and further re-organisation, the First Regiment of Foot Guards. It was their defeat of Napoleon's Imperial Guard at Waterloo which won them re-designation as the First or Grenadier Regiment of Foot Guards, which became shortened to Grenadier Guards. They were also the first Guards Regiments to wear the distinctive bearskin cap.

The Coldstream Guards are named after the small town on the English/Scottish border where they were garrisoned after their Civil War activities as part of Oliver Cromwell's 'New Model Army'. Two years after Cromwell's death, they entered London, under Colonel Monck, in an attempt to bring about calm in a tense situation and were responsible to some great degree for bringing about the elections that created the Parliament which asked King Charles II to return. Though the King, for obvious reasons, disbanded Cromwell's army in 1661, the mounted unit of the regiment were merged into the Life Guards, and in 1670 the foot guards were granted what had become practically their designated name, the Coldstream Guards. The regiment remains the only one in the British army with a direct descent from the Parliamentary Army of the Protectorate.

The Scots Guards were first raised in 1662 by Charles II, although there are some who maintain that the Royal Regiment raised by his father, Charles I, in 1642 as a personal Body Guard and were subsequently disbanded by Oliver Cromwell, were the true antecedents. Which ever way one adheres, their disbanding does account for their ranking third in the Foot Guards. Their 92 Battle Honours, however, attest to their historic motto: *Nemo Me Impune Lacessit*

(No One Provokes Me with Impunity). The Irish Guards were raised, at the instigation of Queen Victoria in April 1900. The Queen had wished to show her appreciation of the part played by Irish soldiers in the Second Boer War. They remain the only regiment in the Household Division who are allowed to have their mascot – an Irish Wolfhound – lead them on parade. The Welsh Guards were raised in February 1915 by George V, and its nucleus was formed by Welshmen from the other regiments of the Foot Guards. By September the same year, the First Battalion, Welsh Guards, fought at Loos and remained a part of the Guards Division for the rest of that war.

Until the creation in 1689, of a regular standing army to be controlled by parliament, it was the monarch who owned the army. The King commanded it and it ranked as a department of the Royal Household. Charles II returned to London in 1660 with three Troops of Horse Guards, six hundred in number. When Charles I had lost the Civil War, Prince Charles, his son, had entered exile in France and the Low Countries with a remnant of noblemen and gentlemen royalists, eighty in all, who became the Life Guards of the Horse. Twenty of them were to guard the exiled King at all times. After the Restoration, the main function of the Life Guards were to guard the Royal Palace in Whitehall and to provide a constant escort for the King as he went about his royal progress. (It is instructive, perhaps, to consider the fate of Louis XIV's Maison du Roi, the French military royal household of 'guards and garrisons' who were the model for King Charles's Life Guards of the Horse. Mounting a guard and providing an escort for The Queen, still remain the major task of the Household Cavalry. While Versailles does not continue the tradition.)

Charles II was aware that the Restoration was, in some quarters, very unpopular. The need to quell the Fifth Monarchist rising in London in 1661 caused the reorganization of the various remnants of the armies, who had fought each other not that long before. The formation in 1660 of the 1st Foot Guards, later to be called the Grenadier Guards, and the re-engagement of Monck's Regiment of Foot, the Coldstream Guards, were merged with Charles II's Life Guard and Cromwell's old Life Guard, the Regiment of the Horse, which would be reformed as the Royal Horse Guards, the Blues. It would cost Charles £122,407.15s.10d. every year to maintain his regiments, around ten per cent of the annual income granted him by parliament.

Defending the Monarch would remain a vital role for all four Regiments, but integrating into the wider military requirements of maintaining Britain's imperial ambitions would also become necessary. The Battle of Maestricht in 1673 was the first campaign fought by the Life Guards. They took decisive action in defeating the Duke of Monmouth, Charles II's bastard son, at Sedgemoor in 1685. They fought against the exiled James II at the Battle of the Boyne in 1690 and fought for King William III, against the French, at Landen. They earned Battle Honours at Waterloo and continued the heroic tradition by gaining 28 Battle Honours in World War I and 21 in World War II.

The same demands would be made of the Royal Horse Guards. When Charles II created 'The Royal Regiment of the Horse' in 1661 from Cromwell's Regiment of the Horse, he gave its command to the Earl of Oxford. Aubrey de Verre, Earl of Oxford, maintained a blue livery for his servants and the new Regiment responded in kind by wearing blue coats. Indeed when King William III, whose 'Glorious Revolution' had such long-reaching affect on nearly all English institutions, and doubting allegiances brought his own Dutch Horse Guards with him, the nick-name 'Oxford Blues' was used to differentiate which Regiment was where. Created the Royal Horse Guards Blue in 1750, they became the Royal Horse Guards (The Blues) in 1819. A year later, in recognition of their bravery at Waterloo and as an honour for their Colonel, the Duke of Wellington, the Blues were given the rank of Household Cavalry, a status only granted till then to the Life Guards.

The Royal Dragoons, the other component of the Blues and Royals, were raised in 1661, when the Earl of Peterborough created the Tangier Horse as the cavalry regiment within the garrison at Tangier. Tangier had been a Portuguese colony since 1471, but Charles II acquired it, along with Bombay, in 1661 as part of the dowry of Catherine of Braganza. It was not a happy place. Poorly defended and in need of considerable fortification, the tensions between the remnants from Cromwell's New Model Army, the ex-royalists from the now defunct Dunkirk garrison and a sturdy group of Irish Catholics were exacerbated by bad conditions, disease and a highly effective local guerilla campaign led by the Moorish leader, Abd Allah Ghailan. Drunkenness was the curse of Tangier 'liberally taken by all sorts as an antidote to drive away sorrow'. By 1684 the garrison was evacuated, and though no one was dismayed to see it go, the possible mercantile and military benefits of a military base in that part of the Mediterranean was not forgotten. Gibraltar was captured in 1704 and kept at the Peace of Utrecht in 1714. By then the regiment, returned to England, was named His Majesty's Own Royal Regiment of Dragoons, and would enjoy a heroic career comparable with the Life Guards. In 1751, the regiment was called the 1st (Royal) Dragoons until 1920, when they were named the 1st the Royal Dragoons. Then, in 1961, the name changed yet again to the Royal Dragoons (1st Dragoons) which they stayed until their amalgamation with the Royal Horse Guards in 1969.

They fought in all the major European wars, from the War of the Spanish Succession, through the Peninsula War and fought, alongside the Life Guards, at Waterloo. They fought in the Crimea, Egypt and South Africa and served without their horses, on foot, in the World War I trenches. Mechanised by World War II, they fought in the Western Desert and North-West Europe and won battle honours in the Falkland Islands.

When the Household Cavalry Regiment was formed in 1992, two squadrons of Life Guards and two squadrons of Blues and Royals were based at Windsor. The union of the Household Cavalry enabled those squadrons equipped with armoured vehicles to be based at Windsor – they did sterling work, alongside the Castle staff and the Duke of York, during the night of the terrible fire that did such appalling damage to the ancient building. One squadron from both the Life Guards and the Blues and Royals are quartered at the barracks in Knightsbridge. These are the

mounted element to the Household Cavalry and are an integral part of the London scene, riding resplendent through the busy traffic as they perform their guard and escort duties for their Colonel-in-Chief.

The Household Cavalry wear full dress uniform whilst performing their task of being The Queen's Life Guard, and when they participate in other occasions of State. The Sovereign's Standard of the Life Guards is carried by the Sovereign's Escort on all State occasions; the Royal Arms, above a listing of the Regiment's main Battle Honours, sewn in gold, red, white and blue silk against a red background and surrounded with gold tassel. The Life Guards wear white-metal helmets, dating from the 1840s, with plumes made from horsehair, scarlet tunics with white leather breeches and white cross-belts with a red flash-cord, worn over the left shoulder. The trumpeters and drummers, always mounted on grey horses, wear a splendid red and gold tunic, richly embroidered, in a pattern and design which was originally made in the reign of Charles II.

The Blue and Royals will also wear full dress uniforms when providing The Queen's Life Guard and attending State occasions. They wear blue tunics, with white leather breeches, red plumes on the same identical helmets as the Life Guards, and both regiments wear the same knee-length black leather boots with wide flaps to protect the knee. Still known as 'Jackboots', the design was from a pattern created by the Prince Regent in 1812. Even the horses still ride with metal links across their necks, a reminder of when a sword-swipe could cut away the bridle and leave the rider vulnerable. Elbow-length white leather gloves, waist high silver swords and saddles covered with black sheepskin, complete a set of historic and elegant uniforms, now worn to be captured by thousands of video-cameras, rather than lost on the fields of battle.

*Left:
The King's
Troop leave
the Windsor
Show Ground
with the
floodlit
castle in the
background*

The last horse regiment with an intimate role to play in the great occasions of state is the Royal Horse Artillery. Formed as two troops in 1793, as the first branch of the Artillery in which all the ranks were to be mounted, the regiment was originally disbanded in 1816, after the end of the Napoleonic wars. The troops were not kept dormant for very long.

It was not until 1716 that the British army acquired an artillery force that was to be permanent. The Jacobite rebellion of 1715 had shown the impracticality of organizing a royal warrant to establish a train of artillery in time; the artillery was not ready for service until the rebellion had been suppressed. Two companies of field artillery were established, by royal warrant, at Woolwich, and as the nature of warfare changed and especially the need to provide heavy fire support for the cavalry, the increasing importance of mobility in battle turned troops into batteries.

By the 1850s the now-named Royal Regiment of Artillery had established 29 batteries of horse artillery, and was brought under the control of the War Office. In 1899 the regiment was split into two, called the Royal Horse and Royal Field Artillery and the Royal Garrison Artillery. Merged in 1924 into one, the Royal Regiment of Artillery, the Royal Horse Artillery would still retain its identity. In 1945, at the express request of King George VI, a mounted battery of the Royal Horse Artillery was re-formed as The Riding Troop, RHA, which became, in 1947, the King's Troop, RHA. Though it ranks as second in precedence to the Household Cavalry, on parade with its guns, the King's Troop has precedence over all other regiments and corps, including the Household Cavalry.

The Queen is their Captain-General and their absence of battle honours is simply that their motto, *Ubique* (Everywhere) was recognized in 1833 as all-embracing. Their uniform is blue with scarlet facings and amongst their nicknames are 'Right of the Line' and the 'Four-Wheeled Hussars'. The King's Troop customarily finds The Queen's Guard in London when the Household Cavalry is at summer camp and always provides the official 21-gun salute on Royal birthdays and state visits. Their horses, whose manes are always shaved, are customarily named after characters from the books of Robert Smith Surtees. A journalist and novelist who managed to become High Sheriff of Durham, Surtees started the *New Sporting Magazine* in 1831; created the sporting cockney, John Jorrocks in *Jorrock's Jaunts and Jollities* (1838) and Mr Soapy Sponge in *Sponge's Sporting Tour* (1853). Both should outlive *Harry Potter*.

The very real dangers and epic splendour of the King's Troop Drive is vividly conveyed in a memory of an occasion at the Royal Windsor Horse Show, when the Drive was to be the spectacular end to the day's events. The Drive is a stupendous spectacle; six six-horse gun-teams charge the length and breadth of the Home Park at flat-out gallop. Performed at dusk, against the floodlit battlements of Windsor Castle, as the salvos blast and the smoke rises up in the evening air, the King's Troop leave the show ring as fast as they entered it. The Drive has often been performed there, though one year, as Bill Lithgow, in Alan Smith's history of the Royal Windsor Horse Show, recalls:

'...Geoffrey Cross moved the ring up a bit, leaving a substantial tree in the middle of the exit, some forty or fifty yards back from the side of the ring. There was still plenty of room, and at our rehearsal I told the drivers to leave the tree on their left so that if their guns skidded they would hit the paling fence rather than the tree. The rehearsal went well and out went the first four teams at a great gallop. Then suddenly to my horror the last two slowed right up. Fearing the worst, I rushed off to look, and it transpired that the lead driver of the fourth team had been run away with and in the last stride changed his mind about the tree – his leaders went to the left and so did the Centres, but the wheelers went each side of it, and the gun, of course, up it.

'The harness, designed as it is for emergencies, gave way and the team horses were virtually unmarked and fit again for the following night. Most sadly the centre of the three gun detachment horses following close behind the gun galloped into it and we had to put him down. The Lead Driver – a veteran of some three and twenty summers – sent for his Centre and Wheel Drivers, mere striplings of nineteen and twenty, and, as he himself told me, said to them, 'Have you lost confidence in me?' to which they replied instantly, 'No Sir, No Sir,' and the following night went out if anything, even faster.

'The tree, with its bark off, remains for all to see.'

· CHAPTER SIX ·

CEREMONIAL

'Militarism is a vexed word... Two definitions are helpful here. [It] can indicate the army's intervention in civilian politics [or] describe the situation where the veneration of things military goes beyond that appropriate to the necessities of warfare... The fact that loyalties are directed towards the regiment and not to the profession at large has contributed to [a] political quiescence. Furthermore, the regiment, with its attention to dress distinctions, to bands, to its own peculiar customs, has been the repository of that second form of militarism, which has thus been dispersed.'

Hew Strachan: *Oxford History of the British Army*

The British standing army was created in 1661, and each regiment was called after the name of its current colonel. There have been many changes since then. In 1881, as Britain's imperial ambitions grew (there was a Persian saying: 'If you trip over a pebble, you can be certain that an Englishman put it there'), 31 cavalry and 113 infantry regiments were required; by the 1980s the number had shrunk to 16 regiments of armour and 39 regiments of infantry. One constant, however, has been the

*The Queen turns towards the Duke of Edinburgh
during the 1961 Trooping the Colour Ceremony*

requirement that the monarch and his or her immediate family provide the Colonel-in-Chief for each and every regiment. The soldiers' oath is sworn first to their monarch, and then their country. It is this historic, almost mystical, allegiance to crown, country and regiment which has such manifest significance in the major ceremonial of any royal year; the annual Trooping the Colour ceremony, 'the greatest parade of all'.

The Sovereign's Birthday Parade, or Trooping the Colour, is held on the day which is determined as the monarch's Official Birthday, always in June. It is held by the Household Division at Horse Guard's Parade, just along the Mall from Buckingham Palace. In good time, before the grand day, special seats are constructed around the parade ground for the many officials, politicians, diplomats and important relatives who attend, as well as more ordinary folk who can watch from vantage points along the route. It is also made available, like some grand sporting event, to television viewers around the world.

In fact, the ceremony's origin is based on a fundamental factor in regimental warfare – the ability to recognise clearly one's regimental colours. When Richard III led his knights in the charge at the Battle of Bosworth, the last English monarch to lead his troops into battle from the front, there was no need to register where and when a soldier fought. It was a tradition of warfare which spread back centuries. Ancient Greeks charged into each other with such ferocity that hundreds of men died standing up, crushed together in the furious centre of the battle.

As armies became larger and divisions within those armies began to perform differing functions on the battlefield, and as the nature of warfare changed with new weapons, the ability of the soldier to know where he belonged could only be determined by finding his flag. In order to ensure this, at the end of every day, each unit's flag, or Colour, would be paraded, or 'trooped' in front of the assembled men and escorted to wherever it was to be kept that night. The same activity would take place, in reverse, every morning. 'Lodging the Colour' would come to assume a reverence which allowed each regiment to honour its past and present in a simple, yet highly symbolic, ceremony.

Along with the establishment of the standing army, when Charles II's ascendancy restored the monarchy, it become necessary to place the various troops in garrison towns. As it became important for the monarch to travel around the kingdom, if for no other reason than to be seen, a Guard would be placed over him (or her) in each town and a parade would take place which came to be known as 'Trooping the Colour'. (It is interesting, perhaps, to note here that the same ceremony is still performed, usually in May, when The Queen's Guard is mounted from Horse Guards.)

When the monarch began to give his or her guards a small gratuity whenever it was his or her birthday, it would become necessary to ensure that the entire brigade

The Queen salutes as the Guards march past Buckingham Palace, Trooping the Colour, 1970

of guards would be given the chance to receive the royal bounty as well. Envy amongst the troops of unequal largesse was not good for morale. And so it came about that these two military traditions would weave into the one fabric of the Sovereign's Birthday Parade, Trooping the Colour.

Each year, by the time The Queen has arrived from Buckingham Palace, alongside members of the Royal Family, escorted by the Sovereign's Escort of the Household Cavalry, at 11am on the dot, six Guards from the Foot, made up of 3 officers and 70 assorted ranks, have been dressed, formed and officers fallen in. The 6th Guard, who have The Queen's Colour, stands at a right-angle to the other five, with the Massed Bands, Pipes and Drums of the Household Cavalry formed up with their backs to the Prime Minister's garden at 10, Downing Street.

After The Queen has inspected the parade, the Massed Bands, Pipes and Drums advance towards the Colour, and back, in slow and fast time. The Drum Majors of the Foot Guards wear a State Dress livery similar in colour to that of the Household Cavalry, with the addition of a gold-fringed crimson apron, and it is always a drummer who will uncase the colour before its escort can troop it, from left to right down along the entire line of Guards.

The Queen on Burmese, Trooping the Colour, 1981

All the Guards now march past The Queen, in slow and fast time, whilst the Colour is brought and lowered in Salute as it passes. The Massed Bands, Pipes and Drums play their loudest, as the Guards reform and it becomes the turn of the Household Cavalry to pass The Queen, once at the walk, next at the trot, dipping their Standard as they do so. The last order of the parade, 'Royal Salute – Present Arms', rings out. The National Anthem is played and everyone reforms to march back up along the Mall, with The Queen's Guard for that day, always at the rear. The Queen heads these Guards on her way back to the Palace, but goes to the Centre Gate in order to witness the Old Guard and the New pass her by, ending the ceremony with The Sovereign's Escort riding past.

For many years The Queen rode a large black horse named Burmese. She would sit, side-saddle, throughout the entire ceremony, which can last nearly three hours; a considerable feat of endurance and equestrian skill. On her 60th birthday parade, whilst riding down the Mall towards the parade ground, a man pointed a revolver directly at her and fired some shots in the direction of her face. As it happened, the gun was not real and the shots were loud caps. For those many thousands watching

Taking the salute, Trooping the Colour, June 1981

The Queen returning to Buckingham Palace, Trooping the Colour, June 1988

the event on television, the shots were clearly audible as was a subtle and barely-noticeable shift in The Queen's composure. Her horse reared slightly, she settled the animal down and continued her ride. The Duke of Edinburgh rode up from behind, but moved back after a brief word with The Queen. The television commentary made no reference to what had happened and many viewers must have thought they had witnessed some apparition. It was only later that day that reference was made to the event, and even then, little information was given out about the man and why he had done what he did.

'The risks of our trade', said Napoleon III to his blood-splattered wife, Eugenie, after an anarchist bomb had been hurled at them. And what a trade!

This brief text wishes to be, above all else, a celebration of one woman, with an extraordinary destiny, whose eventual station in life was never to be that of her own choosing. In this Golden Jubilee year, a narrative which seeks to describe, in an uncontroversial manner, what is clearly an uncomplicated and simple love of horses, combined with a rare gift to understand, breed and ride them, is probably not the best place to ponder for too long the rather complicated issues of monarchy and constitution.

However, as we watch the splendour of The Queen's horses and men riding past, or are charmed by the beauty of the Gold Coronation Coach, there should be time to ponder that the tradition and history of British royal spectacle is more than a grander version of a Hollywood romantic epic about some 19th century middle-European kingdom.

When The Queen ascended the throne, there was much talk of a new Elizabethan age. A well-respected children's monthly journal, owned by a distinguished Scottish publishing dynasty changed its name from *Collin's Children's Magazine* to the *Young Elizabethan*. Benjamin Britten wrote a now rarely performed opera, *Gloriana*, which premiered at the Royal Opera House, Covent Garden. 1953 came to be known simply as 'Coronation Year'.

At the time, there seemed a profound need, certainly in the press and elsewhere, to link the new monarch with her earlier namesake, Elizabeth I. 'You may well have a greater prince,' said our good Queen Bess after the defeat of the Spanish Armada, 'but you shall never have a more loving prince'. Queen Elizabeth II was reported to have said she did not feel like her Tudor forebear 'who was blessed with neither husband nor children, who ruled as a despot and was never able to leave her shores', yet there was a sense in the air, at the time, of liberation and celebration, which amounted to love of something, even if there was an ambiguity about what it was. And though *Tribune*, the radical newspaper, would write: 'It really should be possible to crown a constitutional monarch in a democratic country without giving the impression that Britain has been transformed into Ruritania', the event itself provoked parties and celebrations across the land, the like of which had not been seen since before both world wars.

Yet 'Coronation Year' was also a time when the entire press contingent, who were covering Princess Elizabeth's trip to Kenya, had stood in silence with their cameras 'limp in their left hands and their right hands held over their hearts', when having been told the awful news of her father's death, and now Queen, she had left for the

President Ronald Reagan and Queen Elizabeth II ride at Windsor, June 1982

sad flight home. And though our now mostly intrusive press may simply reflect their customers' wish for a more intrusive culture, we might do well to remember that in the year when George V decided to admit innocent parties in divorce proceedings to the royal enclosure at Ascot (the decision would be regarded as daringly enlightened) the woman whose Golden Jubilee we celebrate had just been featured on the front cover, aged three, of *Time*. 'Such times we've seen. Such times...' indeed!

The Queen's grandfather, after receiving a huge ovation on his Silver Jubilee trip into the East End of London, told the then Archbishop of Canterbury about his amazement: 'But I cannot understand,' said the King, 'I am quite an ordinary sort of fellow'. To which the prelate replied, 'Yes, Sir, that is just it'. John Updike in a *New Yorker* book review on one of the many books about The Queen, remembers 'Chesterton somewhere wrote that a democracy and a monarchy are alike in proposing that any man is fit to rule'.

Of course, dissent against the monarch is almost as old as the monarchy. Take Shelley, in his first few lines of *England in 1819*, going straight for the jugular, (and also quoted by Updike):

> An old, mad, blind, despised, and dying king,–
> Princes, the dregs of their dull race, who flow
> Through public scorn, – mud from a muddy spring, –
> Rulers who neither see, nor feel, nor know,
> But leech-like to their fainting country cling,
> Till they drop, blind in blood, without a blow ...'

Yet, in the end, it is the continuity of things, both good and bad, both for and against, that count in the story of any nation. As the horse breeder will back her bloodlines because of experience and continuity, so to a nation must attempt to understand the link between past and present.

Peter Vansittart ends his excellent book, *In Memory of England*, by quoting the playwright Dennis Potter's assertion that 'the noblest task of the popular historian should be to make us ashamed of our forefathers'. Vansittart's conclusion expresses a sentiment about the telling of stories which has hopefully been achieved by this small contribution to a very special occasion. He ends, '...but ... getting History wrong is an essential part of being a nation ... even if most of our popular history is a self-regarding tall story, I like to think that the gist of it was worth the telling'.

Acknowledgements

The publishers wish to thank the following for
their help in the preparation of this book:

The Royal Windsor Horse Show
Simon Brooks-Ward
Rushman Communications Ltd
Keith Prowse Hospitality Ltd

Photograph Credits:

The Royal Windsor Horse Show
Kit Houghton Photography
Camera Press
Hulton Getty
Mirror Group Newspapers
Corbis

Published in Great Britain by

AQS Publishing Ltd
Camfield Place
Hatfield
Herts Al09 6JE

Text © 2002 David Elliott

ISBN 1 872571 06 9

First Edition

Book Design by Brad Thompson
Cover Photography by Kit Houghton Photography
Printed by Victoria Litho, London
Bound by MPG Printers, Bodmin